Cook & Color

by Shelley Zarenda

Cook & Color

by
Shelley Zarenda

First Printing – March 1995

Cooking For Kids
1012 Rick Hansen Crescent
Kingston, Ontario
K7P 2M8

Canadian Cataloguing in Publication Data

Zarenda, Shelley, 1973 -

Cook & color

Includes index.
ISBN 1-895292-52-2

1. Cookery – Juvenile literature. 2. Coloring books.
I. Title.

TX652.5.Z37 1995 jC641.5"123 C95-920070-3

Illustrations by
Cheryl Kaplan
Shelley Zarenda

Designed, Printed and Produced in Canada by:
Centax Books, a Division of PrintWest Communications Ltd.
Publishing Director: Margo Embury
1150 Eighth Avenue
Regina, Saskatchewan
Canada S4R 1C9
(306) 525-2304 FAX (306) 757-2439

Table of Contents

Recipes have been tested in U.S. Standard measurements. Common metric measurements are given as a convenience for those who are more familiar with metric. Recipes have not been tested in metric.

Depending on each child's cooking experience, parental supervision may be required for some of the recipes.

Recipes are coded: EASY: 🍦
MEDIUM: 🍦 🍦
HARD: 🍦 🍦 🍦

Food For Thought

Looking back on my childhood, it is little wonder that I am so enthusiastic about food and its preparation. My grandmother has always baked the most wonderful cakes and cookies, and my mother is a food lover's dream. She is a wonderful cook and baker. She has been in the catering business and has published a marvelous recipe book. My dad and brother love food and are always available for taste-testing. Growing up in this environment really sparked my interest in cooking and baking.

As a young child I would stand at my mother's side hoping she would let me add a spoonful of sugar or sift the flour. While I was growing up, my mother sent me to cooking courses. This further stimulated my interest and increased my involvement in food preparation in our home. A few years later I became my mother's chief taster, as she worked hard preparing her baking recipes for publishing. I also helped her with her catering, and this gave me an insight into food preparation and presentation.

After a few years of home economics at high school, I had learnt more about food groups, cooking methods, terms and rules. I was also invited to be in charge of catering for our graduation formal, which gave me valuable experience in all aspects of food.

A year later my family moved from South Africa to Canada. I got a counselling job at a summer camp and the following year I decided to accept a specialist position . . . head of cooking classes. I ran this activity many times a day and it became very popular. I enjoyed seeing kids between the ages of 7 to 12 having fun and learning at the same time. We put together our own recipes, learned to substitute for missing or allergic ingredients, and I was able to learn which recipes appealed most to kids of this age group.

At the end of that summer, I decided that the most positive way I could use my experiences was to produce a special recipe book. This book includes simple recipes, as well as appealing pictures for kids to color, an unusual idea to keep the young "chefs" busy while waiting for the food to bake, cook or cool.

I hope you get as much fun out of the book as I had putting it all together.

Love, Shelley

Rules For The Cook

- Wash your hands and put on an apron before you begin cooking.
- When choosing a recipe, be sure to notice that the recipes are coded in relation to difficulty. Choose one that is right for you or ask a more experienced cook to help you.
- Read through the ingredients, methods and hints of the recipe before beginning.
- If there are any words that you do not know, look them up in the glossary.
- Set out the utensils and ingredients to make sure that you have everything that you need.
- To lessen the mess at the end, clean up as you go along.
- Be extra careful when handling knives and other sharp objects.
- Turn the handles of pots and pans towards the wall so that you will not accidentally knock them off the stove.
- Electric switches should be touched only with dry hands.
- Working with boiling water, oil and syrups can be very dangerous. Always have an adult to help you with these.
- Remember to use oven mitts when you are handling things from the oven.
- Before placing hot pans on the counter, put a wooden board or heatproof pad on the counter so the surface won't be burned.
- All appliances, including the oven, should be turned off before leaving the kitchen.
- After washing up, put everything back where you found it.

Hints and Tips

Cracking and Separating Eggs:

- Holding an egg in one hand, tap the middle of the egg firmly on the rim of a bowl. Put your thumbs on either side of the crack and pull the shell apart over the bowl.
- To separate the yolk from the white, put a large mesh strainer over a small bowl. Carefully crack the egg and slide it into the strainer. The egg white will go through the strainer into the bowl. Lift the strainer and drop the yolk into a separate bowl.

Brownies and Squares:

- Use the pan size specified in the recipe.
- If you do not have the specified size, use a smaller pan rather than a larger one. You may have to increase the cooking time.
- If the pan is too large the mixture will be spread too thin and it will burn.
- To stop squares from crumbling, cut when completely cool.

Freezing Cookies:

- Unfrosted cookies can be stored in an airtight container for up to 9 months with the layers separated with waxed paper.
- Frosted cookies can be stored in an airtight container for up to 3 months.
- To thaw, let cookies stand, uncovered, at room temperature.

Problems With Dough – To Fix:

- If the dough is too dry and does not hold together well enough, add 1-2 tbsp. (15-30 mL) of milk.
- If the dough is too soft, fix it by working in 1 tbsp. (15 mL) of flour at a time until it is stiff enough.

Chocolate:

- Milk chocolate, chocolate mint and semisweet chocolate chips can be used interchangeably.

Cookie Painting:

- Combine 1 egg yolk and 1/4 tsp. (1 mL) water, add food coloring. Paint the unbaked cookies with a paintbrush and bake.

Margarine and Butter:

- These are interchangeable in the same quantities for most recipes – the texture and flavor may differ – especially in recipes like shortbread cookies. Light, diet or whipped margarine can not be used for baking.
- A dough that is made of butter becomes firmer in the refrigerator than a dough made from spreadable margarine.

Measurements:

¼ tsp. = 1 mL	¼ cup = 60 mL	1¼ cups = 300 mL
½ tsp. = 2 mL	⅓ cup = 75 mL	1½ cups = 375 mL
1 tsp. = 5 mL	½ cup = 125 mL	1¾ cups = 425 mL
2 tsp. = 10 mL	⅔ cup = 150 mL	2 cups = .5 L or 500 mL
1 tbsp. = 15 mL	¾ cup = 175 mL	4 cups = 1 L or 1000 mL
2 tbsp. = 30 mL	1 cup = 250 mL	

Metric Baking Temperatures:

120°C = 250°F	220°C = 425°F
140°C = 275°F	230°C = 450°F
150°C = 300°F	240°C = 475°F
160°C = 325°F	260°C = 500°F
180°C = 350°F	270°C = 525°F
200°C = 400°F	290°C = 500°F

Glossary

Bake: to cook by dry heat in an oven.

Baking Tray: a cookie sheet.

Beat: to mix rapidly with a spoon, whisk or beater until a mixture is smooth.

Boil: to heat a liquid on the stove until bubbles appear on the surface and break open.

Chop: to use a knife to cut food into small pieces.

Cream: to make butter soft and smooth by mixing with a spoon or beater.

Dash: slightly more than a pinch (see below), the amount sprinkled from a spice shaker or bottle in 1 sharp downward shake.

Fry: to cook something in a pan with hot oil. Deep-frying needs the oil deep enough to cover the food.

Grease: use paper towel, waxed paper or the butter or margarine wrapper to smear fat over the inside of a pan.

Grate/Shred: to make small bits or long, thin strips of foods, e.g., chocolate, cheese, cucumbers, carrots, etc. Metal or plastic graters have sharp-edged, large, medium or small holes.

Icing Sugar: confectioner's sugar or powdered sugar.

Mash: to press something down with a fork or potato masher to remove all of the lumps.

Mix: to combine all of the ingredients until they are evenly distributed.

Peel: to strip off or pull away the outer covering of a fruit or vegetable.

Pinch: about 1⁄16 of a teaspoon (0.25 mL), the amount held between thumb and forefinger tips.

Preheat: to turn the oven on and give it time to reach a certain temperature before cooking.

Sift: to put the dry ingredients, such as flour, through a fine strainer or sifter.

Stir: to mix the ingredients in a circular motion.

Whip: to beat rapidly, using a wire whisk or egg beater, to incorporate air, lighten the mixture and increase its volume.

breads
'n
MUFFINS

Cheese Muffins

Quick and Easy.

2 cups	**shredded Cheddar cheese**	**500 mL**
1 cup	**flour**	**250 mL**
2½ tsp.	**baking powder**	**12 mL**
½ tsp.	**dry mustard**	**2 mL**
1	**egg**	**1**
¾ cup	**milk**	**175 mL**

1. Preheat oven to 450°F (230°C).
2. Mix cheese and all dry ingredients together in a medium bowl.
3. Beat the egg in a cup, and use the ¾ cup (175 mL) of milk to fill the cup.
4. Add egg mixture to dry ingredients and mix well.
5. Grease a muffin pan, and spoon in the batter until the cups are ¾ full.
6. Bake for 10-15 minutes. See the baking hint on page 11 to test if muffins are ready.
7. Remove muffins from the oven, and allow to cool before removing from the pan and eating.

Yield: 12 medium muffins

Banana Muffins

These are Mom's best.

2	**medium bananas**	**2**
½	**beaten egg***	**½**
½ cup	**sugar**	**125 mL**
¼ cup	**butter**	**60 mL**
¾ cup	**flour**	**175 mL**
1 tsp.	**baking soda**	**5 mL**
pinch	**salt**	**pinch**

1. Preheat oven to 350°F (180°C).
2. Mash bananas on a flat plate.
3. In a medium bowl, combine egg and sugar.
4. Add banana to egg and sugar mixture.
5. Melt butter over medium heat, then add to banana mixture.
6. In another bowl, sift together dry ingredients.
7. Add dry ingredients to banana mixture, and mix gently until barely combined.
8. Grease muffin pan, and spoon in the batter until the cups are ⅔ full.
9. Bake for 20-25 minutes.
10. Remove from oven, and allow to cool before removing from the pan and eating.

Yield: 6 medium muffins or 12 minimuffins

*Beat a whole egg in a measuring cup and spoon half of it into the sugar. Discard the remaining half egg.

Baking Hint: It is always good to test if a baked good is ready by taking a metal skewer, a toothpick or a sharp knife and poking it into the baked product near the center. If the object comes out clean, it is ready. If the object comes out dirty, it is not ready!

Chocolate Muffins

¾ cup	**flour**	**175 mL**
¼ cup	**sugar**	**60 mL**
1½ tsp.	**baking powder**	**7 mL**
pinch	**salt**	**pinch**
1½ tbsp.	**cocoa powder**	**22 mL**
½ cup	**semisweet chocolate chips**	**125 mL**
½	**beaten egg (see note on page 11)**	**½**
2½ tbsp.	**melted margarine**	**37 mL**
½ cup	**milk**	**125 mL**

1. Preheat oven to 375°F (190°C).
2. In a medium bowl, mix together dry ingredients.
3. Add chocolate chips to dry ingredients.
4. In a separate bowl, mix together the egg, margarine and milk.
5. Add dry ingredients to egg mixture and mix well.
6. Grease a muffin pan, and spoon in the batter until the muffin cups are ⅔ full.
7. Bake for 20-25 minutes. See the baking hint on page 11 to test if muffins are ready.
8. Remove from oven, and allow to cool before removing from the pan and eating.

Yield: 10 minimuffins

Chocolate Cupcakes

Dreamy!!

1½ cups	**flour**	**375 mL**
1 cup	**sugar**	**250 mL**
¼ cup	**cocoa powder**	**60 mL**
1 tsp.	**baking soda**	**5 mL**
1 cup	**water**	**250 mL**
⅓ cup	**vegetable oil**	**75 mL**
1 tbsp.	**cider vinegar**	**15 mL**
1 tsp.	**vanilla extract**	**5 mL**
½ cup	**cream cheese, softened**	**125 mL**
1	**egg**	**1**
¼ cup	**sugar**	**60 mL**
pinch	**salt**	**pinch**
¾ cup	**chocolate chips**	**175 mL**

1. Preheat oven to 350°F (180°C).
2. Grease a muffin pan.
3. Sift the flour, sugar, cocoa powder and baking powder together in a medium bowl.
4. In a small bowl, combine water, oil, vinegar and vanilla extract; add to dry ingredients.
5. Mix with an electric beater at medium speed for 3 minutes.
6. For the filling, in another bowl, mix together cream cheese, egg, sugar and salt; beat until smooth.
7. Stir in the chocolate chips.
8. Fill each muffin cup ⅔ full with chocolate batter.
9. Put 2 tsp. (10 mL) of chocolate chip filling on top of each cupcake.
10. Bake for 20-25 minutes, or until cupcakes spring back when lightly touched.
11. Allow to cool in the pan and then remove and . . . enjoy!

Yield: 10-12 medium cupcakes

Banana Bread

Very basic and very good!

1¼ cups	**flour**	**300 mL**
1 tsp.	**baking soda**	**5 mL**
2	**eggs, lightly beaten**	**2**
½ cup	**oil**	**125 mL**
1 cup	**sugar**	**250 mL**
2	**ripe bananas, mashed**	**2**
¼ cup	**chopped nuts or chocolate chips**	**60 mL**

1. Preheat oven to 350°F (180°C).
2. In a medium bowl, sift the flour and baking soda together and stir until completely mixed.
3. In a small bowl, mix together the eggs, oil, sugar, bananas and nuts, add to the flour mixture and stir until blended.
4. Grease a 3 x 5 x 9" (8 x 13 x 23 cm) bread pan.
5. Pour in batter and bake for 1 hour.
6. Remove from oven; allow to cool before removing from pan.

Yield: 1 medium loaf, which freezes well

Basic Butter Cake

⅓ cup	**butter**	**75 mL**
1 cup	**sugar**	**250 mL**
2	**eggs**	**2**
½ tsp.	**vanilla extract**	**2 mL**
2 cups	**flour**	**500 mL**
pinch	**salt**	**pinch**
2½ tsp.	**baking powder**	**12 mL**
½ cup	**water**	**125 mL**

1. Preheat oven to 350°F (180°C).
2. In a small saucepan, melt butter over medium heat.

Basic Butter Cake

Continued

3. In a medium bowl, combine the butter and sugar well.
4. Add eggs 1 at a time, mixing well after the addition of each egg.
5. Add the vanilla extract to the butter mixture.
6. In a separate bowl, sift together flour, salt and baking powder.
7. Into the butter mixture, stir in half the dry ingredients and then half of the water.
8. Stir in the rest of the dry ingredients and the remaining water.
9. Grease a 3 x 5 x 9" (8 x 13 x 23 cm) loaf pan; pour in batter.
10. Bake for 45 minutes-1 hour, until golden brown in appearance.
11. Remove from oven; allow to cool before removing from pan.
12. Frost with the following fabulous butter icing.

Yield: 1 small loaf; 8-10 slices

Butter Icing

A creamy chocolate frosting.

¼ cup	**butter**	**60 mL**
1 tbsp.	**cocoa powder**	**15 mL**
1 cup	**icing sugar**	**250 mL**

1. In a small saucepan, melt the butter and cocoa powder together over medium heat.
2. Remove from heat once it has melted.
3. Stir in icing sugar a little at a time, mixing it in well.
4. If the icing becomes lumpy, add a few drops of boiling water.
5. Place the icing in the refrigerator to stiffen a little so it will spread nicely.
6. This icing can be used to ice cakes, cupcakes or cookies. You can make patterns in it to decorate your baking.

Yield: enough icing for 1 small cake or loaf

Variations: Colorings or flavorings can be used in small amounts instead of the cocoa. Try 1 tsp. (5 mL) lemon extract and a few drops of yellow food coloring, or orange extract and color, or almond extract.

Savory Snacks
PIZZA

Flapjacks

These thick and fluffy pancakes taste good with syrup and ice cream, jam and peanut butter, or just plain butter!

1	**egg**	**1**
⅓ cup	**sugar**	**75 mL**
½ cup	**milk**	**125 mL**
1 cup	**all-purpose flour**	**250 mL**
pinch	**salt**	**pinch**
1 tsp.	**baking powder**	**5 mL**
½ cup	**oil for frying**	**125 mL**

1. In a medium bowl, using an electric mixer, beat egg and sugar together. Add milk and continue beating until well mixed.
2. In a small bowl, sift together the flour and salt.
3. Pour the dry ingredients into the egg mixture and mix with the electric mixer.
4. Lastly, add the baking powder and mix gently.
5. Use a paper towel dipped in oil to grease a frying pan.
6. Place the frying pan over high heat.
7. After a minute, drop a bit of the batter into the pan to see if the pan is ready. If the batter sizzles it is ready.
8. Drop large spoonfuls of the batter into the pan, giving it space to spread.
9. You can usually fit in 4 flapjacks at a time.
10. When bubbles appear on the top, turn the flapjacks over and cook the other side; watch carefully to make sure that they do not burn.
11. Turn off the heat and serve immediately with any of the toppings suggested above.

Yield: 10 medium flapjacks

Variations: For a special weekend breakfast, these are also great with sliced, sweetened strawberries or peaches and a topping of whipped cream.

Real French Toast

3	**eggs**	**3**
⅓ cup	**milk**	**75 mL**
8	**slices day-old bread**	**8**
	margarine	
	syrup	

1. Grease a frying pan with margarine by placing some margarine on a paper towel and spreading the entire surface with the margarine.
2. Heat the pan over medium heat, approximately 375°F (190°C) on an electric frying pan.
3. Mix the eggs and milk in a small shallow bowl, using a fork.
4. Dip 1 piece of bread at a time into the egg mixture.
5. Leave the bread in the bowl for a few seconds, long enough for it to absorb some egg and milk.
6. Cook the bread in the pan for about 4 minutes, then turn the bread over with a pancake turner and allow it to cook 4 minutes longer, until golden brown on both sides.
7. When the first piece is ready, put it on a plate and repeat the whole process with the next piece of bread.
8. When all the cooking is done and you have 8 pieces of French toast stacked on top of each other, warm them in the microwave for a few seconds.
9. Then cover them in loads of syrup and enjoy!

Yield: 8 pieces of French toast, giving 4 really hungry people 2 slices each.

Variations: For a real treat you could top the French toast with blueberries or sliced bananas or strawberries. A sprinkle of cinnamon is also nice with the sliced bananas.

Cheese Bread

Garlic and cheese make this a great flavor combination with spaghetti or soups.

1	**loaf French bread**	**1**
3	**garlic cloves**	**3**
½ cup	**olive oil**	**125 mL**
	a few dashes of salt and pepper	
2 cups	**grated Cheddar or Mozzarella cheese**	**500 mL**

1. Preheat oven to 400°F (200°C).
2. Slice the French bread lengthways (from one end to the other so you have a top and a bottom).
3. Chop the garlic cloves into very small pieces.
4. Add the garlic to the olive oil.
5. Using a basting brush (almost like a paint brush) spread the olive oil along the cut sides of the bread.
6. Sprinkle salt and pepper on both cut sides.
7. Scatter the grated cheese along the bottom half.
8. Cut the bread into 1" (2.5 cm) slices, but do not cut through the bottom of the French bread.
9. Close the bread up with the cheese inside, and wrap in a long piece of aluminum foil.
10. Put on a baking tray and put into the oven.
11. Bake for 15 minutes and then remove from the oven.
12. Allow to cool for about 7 minutes, opening the foil so the steam can escape.
13. Allow each person to pull off a slice.

Yield: 1 loaf

Pizza

There are 3 variations on pizza that are all quick and easy – Pizza Pitas, Pizza Pockets and Pizza Bagels.*

10	**pita breads OR 5 bagels**	**10**
2 cups	**pizza sauce**	**500 mL**
2 cups	**grated mozzarella cheese**	**500 mL**
	sliced pepperoni, mushrooms, tomato, green pepper, onion, olives or pineapple tidbits	

Pizza Pitas

1. Preheat the oven to 400°F (200°C).
2. Place flat pita breads on a baking tray.
3. Drop a few spoonfuls of pizza sauce onto pita breads and spread evenly.
4. Place the toppings you want on top of the sauce.
5. Sprinkle the grated cheese over, place on a cookie sheet and put into the oven.
6. Leave in the oven for 7-10 minutes, or until the cheese has melted.
7. When ready, remove from oven and allow to cool slightly before eating.

Pita Pockets

1. Preheat the oven to 400°F (200°C).
2. Cut a slice off the edge of the pita bread so you can open the pocket.
3. In a bowl, mix the pizza sauce, grated cheese and toppings together.
4. Spoon the mixture inside the pita bread.
5. Place pita breads on a baking tray and put into the oven for 7-10 minutes.
6. Remove and allow to cool slightly before eating.

Pizza

Continued

Pizza Bagels

1. Preheat the oven to 400°F (200°C).
2. Slice the bagels in half and spread each half with pizza sauce.
3. Place the toppings you desire on top, and sprinkle grated cheese over generously.
4. Put the pizza bagels on a baking tray and put into the oven for 7-10 minutes, or until cheese has melted.
5. Remove from oven and allow to cool slightly before eating.

*Each of these methods produces scrumptious results.

Yield: 10 individual "pizzas"

Sandwiches

Use your imagination to make easy and delicious sandwiches. Following are some ideas.

mashed avocado and lemon juice
cream cheese and honey
tuna with mayonnaise and apple or pineapple
peanut butter and jam
grated or sliced Cheddar cheese and tomato
cream or Cheddar cheese and jam
cottage cheese and chopped up fruit (e.g., pineapple, apples)
peanut butter and bananas

1. Combine the ingredients of any of the above combinations. Spread between 2 pieces of bread, or on a bagel or croissant. Simple and Delicious!

Framed Eggs

1	**slice bread**	**1**
1 tsp.	**butter**	**5 mL**
1	**egg**	**1**
	salt and pepper to taste	

1. Take 1 slice of bread and, using a round cookie cutter or the rim of a glass, cut a circle out of the center.
2. Butter both sides of the slice of bread.
3. Grease a small frying pan and place it over medium to high heat.
4. Place the bread in the pan and brown the bottom.
5. When it has browned, turn the bread over and brown the other side.
6. Crack an egg into a cup (to check for defects).
7. Pour the egg into the "frame".
8. Cook until the egg sets and sprinkle with salt and pepper.
9. Remove the frying pan from the heat and place the framed egg on a dish.

Serves: 1

Cookie Jar
crazy
COOKIES

Alphabet Cookies

½ cup	**butter**	**125 mL**
½ cup	**sugar**	**125 mL**
2	**egg yolks**	**2**
½ cup	**ground almonds**	**125 mL**
1-1½ cups	**flour**	**250-375 mL**

1. Preheat oven to 350°F (180°C).
2. In a small saucepan, melt butter over medium heat.
3. Place sugar in a medium bowl; add melted butter and mix well.
4. Add egg yolks and almonds to the sugar mixture.
5. Finally, add the flour, ½ cup (125 mL) at a time, and mix well after each addition. Stop adding the flour when the mixture reaches a dough-like consistency.
6. Break the dough into 10 pieces. Roll dough into long strands and form any letter of the alphabet that you like.
7. Grease a cookie sheet and place the alphabet shapes on it.
8. Do not put them close to each other because they expand as they bake.
9. Place on the middle oven rack and bake for 10-12 minutes, or until golden brown.

Yield: 10 large cookies

Shortbread Balls

½ cup	butter	125 mL
½ tsp.	vanilla extract	2 mL
2 tbsp.	superfine sugar*	30 mL
¼ cup	chopped almonds or peanuts	60 mL
1 cup	all-purpose flour	250 mL
	additional superfine sugar for coating	

1. Preheat oven to 350°F (180°C).
2. In a medium saucepan, melt butter over medium heat.
3. When butter has melted, remove from the heat and add vanilla extract.
4. Add the superfine sugar, chopped nuts and flour.
5. Knead well.
6. Form little balls of the dough.
7. Grease a cookie sheet and place the little dough balls on it.
8. Bake on the middle oven rack for 20-25 minutes, until golden brown.
9. While the cookies are baking, place some additional superfine sugar in a small bowl.
10. Remove cookies from the oven and carefully place the hot balls in the bowl, covering them with the superfine sugar.
11. Remove cookies and allow them to cool on a cooling rack.

Yield: 12 shortbread balls 

*Superfine sugar is also called berry, fruit or castor sugar.

Cinnamon Hearts

Sweet Cookie Dough:

6 tbsp.	**butter**	**90 mL**
½ cup	**sugar**	**125 mL**
1½ cups	**flour***	**375 mL**
pinch	**salt**	**pinch**
1½ tsp.	**baking powder**	**7 mL**
1	**egg**	**1**
2 tbsp.	**milk**	**30 mL**

Sugar Topping:

¼ cup	**sugar**	**60 mL**
2 tsp.	**cinnamon**	**10 mL**
1	**egg**	**1**

1. In a medium saucepan, melt butter over medium heat.
2. When butter has melted, remove from the heat, add the sugar and cream well.
3. Sift the salt, flour and baking powder into a small bowl.
4. With an electric mixer, mix egg and milk together and add to the sugar mixture. Continue mixing well.
5. Add half the dry ingredients to the mixture and mix well.
6. Add the rest of the dry ingredients and begin to use your hands to knead the dough. Make sure your hands are clean! Add a little extra flour if the dough is too sticky.
7. Store dough in a covered container in the refrigerator until you want to use it. It keeps for 2 weeks.
8. Preheat oven to 350°F (180°C).
9. Sprinkle some flour over a board and put a little on the rolling pin.
10. Roll out the dough until it is flat and smooth.
11. Use a heart-shaped cookie cutter to cut shapes out of the dough.

Cinnamon Hearts

Continued

12. Grease a cookie sheet and place the cookies on it.
13. To make the topping, in a small bowl mix together the sugar and the cinnamon.
14. In a cup, beat the egg with a fork.
15. Use a brush to cover each cookie surface with the beaten egg.
16. Using a spoon, sprinkle cinnamon mixture over the egg and bake the cookies on the middle oven rack for 10-15 minutes, until golden brown.
17. When cookies are ready, remove from the oven and lift each one onto a wire cooling rack.

Yield: 14-16 cookies

*Have some extra flour set aside in case the dough is too sticky and also to use when you roll out the cookies.

Variation: Painted Cookies

Follow the recipe to the end of step #10. Cut the dough in any shape you like and bake them as directed, but without the topping. When cookies are cooled, decorate them with Cookie Paints (page 7).

Jam Cupcakes

My Grandmother's specialty.

Base:

1 cup	**butter**	**250 mL**
3 cups	**flour, sifted**	**750 mL**
¾ cup	**sugar**	**175 mL**
pinch	**salt**	**pinch**
2 tsp.	**baking powder**	**10 mL**
2	**eggs**	**2**

Filling:

1 cup	**jam (strawberry or apricot)**	**250 mL**

Topping:

½ cup	**sugar**	**125 mL**
½ cup	**margarine**	**125 mL**
2	**eggs**	**2**
½ cup	**sifted flour**	**125 mL**
1 tsp.	**baking powder**	**5 mL**

1. Preheat the oven to 350°F (180°C).
2. In a large bowl, with clean hands, rub the butter and sifted flour together.
3. Add the sugar, salt and baking powder and continue mixing with your hands.
4. In a small bowl, beat the eggs.
5. Add the eggs to the flour mixture and mix them in with your hands.
6. On a flour-dusted board, roll out the dough until it is smooth and thin.
7. Using a LARGE cup (a coffee mug works well), cut out circles.
8. Grease a large muffin pan and line the metal cups with the dough. Smooth the dough out so that it lines most of the cup.
9. Drop a tablespoon (15 mL) of jam into the center of the cookie dough cup.

Jam Cupcakes

Continued

10. In a medium bowl, combine the sugar, margarine, eggs, sifted flour and baking powder, mixing with an electric beater, to make a topping. Mix well.
11. Place a spoonful of topping on the jam, covering jam completely.
12. Place the muffin pan on the middle oven rack for 15 minutes, or until cupcakes are a golden brown colour.
13. Remove the cupcakes from the pan when they are cool.

*Any extra dough is perfect for a handful of plain cookies, baked on a greased cookie sheet in a 350°F (180°C) oven for 10-12 minutes.

Yield: 12 cupcakes

Gingerbread People

These are fun to make and eat. At Christmas you can use them to decorate your tree or give them as gifts.

2 tbsp.	**butter**	**30 mL**
¼ cup	**brown sugar**	**60 mL**
1	**egg yolk**	**1**
1¼ cups	**all-purpose flour**	**300 mL**
½ tsp.	**baking soda**	**2 mL**
1½ tsp.	**ginger**	**7 mL**
1¼ tbsp.	**corn syrup**	**19 mL**

1. Preheat the oven to 350°F (180°C).
2. In a medium bowl, cream the butter and the sugar until it is light and creamy.
3. Add the egg yolk and continue mixing.
4. Sift the flour, baking soda and ginger into a small bowl.
5. Add the sifted dry ingredients and the corn syrup to the creamy mixture and mix well.
6. Using your hands, in the bowl, knead the dough 10 times.
7. Dust a board and rolling pin lightly with flour.
8. Roll the dough out until it is smooth and thin, about ¼" (6 mm) thick.
9. Using a cookie cutter, cut out the gingerbread people shapes.
10. Grease a cookie sheet and place the cut out shapes on the sheet. You may want to use a cookie lifter so the dough figures do not break.
11. Bake the cookies on the middle oven rack for 10-12 minutes.
12. Remove the cookies from the oven and allow them to cool. Do not decorate until they are completely cool.

Decorating: To decorate these people, you can buy icing tubes or you can use butter icing (page 15) and mix different colors into it. You can also decorate with chocolate sprinkles, licorice, candy-coated chocolate candies and other candies.

Yield: 10 gingerbread people about 6" (15 cm) tall.

Choco Reversals

This recipe is a lot of fun to make.

2 tbsp.	**butter**	**30 mL**
2 tbsp.	**white sugar**	**30 mL**
3 tbsp.	**brown sugar**	**45 mL**
1	**egg yolk**	**1**
3 tbsp.	**all-purpose flour**	**45 mL**
1 tsp.	**baking powder**	**5 mL**
3 tbsp.	**cocoa**	**45 mL**
2 tbsp.	**milk**	**30 mL**
⅔ cup	**rolled oats**	**150 mL**
2 tbsp.	**white chocolate chips**	**30 mL**
2 tbsp.	**dark chocolate chips**	**30 mL**

1. Preheat the oven to 350°F (180°C).
2. In a medium bowl, mix all the ingredients together in the order given.
3. After mixing very well, grease a cookie sheet.
4. Drop by spoonfuls onto the cookie sheet.
5. Place on the middle oven rack for 20-25 minutes.
6. When cookies are ready, remove from the oven and allow them to cool before eating.

Yield: 10 large or 12 medium cookies

Oatmeal Cookies

Brown sugar gives these a rich butterscotch flavor!

1 cup	**oatmeal**	**250 mL**
1 cup	**all-purpose flour**	**250 mL**
½ tsp.	**baking soda**	**2 mL**
pinch	**salt**	**pinch**
½ cup	**butter**	**125 mL**
1 cup	**brown sugar**	**250 mL**
1	**egg**	**1**
1 tsp.	**vanilla extract**	**5 mL**

1. In a small bowl, combine the oatmeal, flour, baking soda and salt.
2. In a medium bowl, cream together butter and sugar.
3. When creamy and smooth, add the egg and vanilla extract.
4. Add the oatmeal mixture to the sugar mixture, and mix very well.
5. Place the dough in a tightly closed container in the refrigerator until it is firm, approximately 1½ hours.
6. Preheat the oven to 400°F (200°C).
7. For large cookies, form round balls the size of golf balls from the dough.
8. Grease a cookie sheet, and place dough balls on the sheet.
9. Use the back of a fork to push down and flatten the balls.
10. Make sure there is enough space between the cookies so that they can expand without touching the others.
11. Place on the middle oven rack for 10-12 minutes.

Yield: 2 dozen large or 3 dozen medium cookies

Superb Squares

No-Bake Squares

½ cup	**butter**	**125 mL**
1 cup	**sugar**	**250 mL**
2 tbsp.	**cocoa powder**	**30 mL**
1	**egg**	**1**
1 tsp.	**vanilla extract**	**5 mL**
10½ oz.	**package Arrowroot cookies**	**300 g**

1. Cream the butter and sugar together until smooth and thick.
2. Add the cocoa powder, egg and vanilla extract and mix well.
3. Crush the arrowroot cookies into small pieces.
4. Add the crushed cookies to the mixture and mix well.
5. Grease an 8" (20 cm) square baking dish and pour the mixture into it.
6. Spread the mixture until it is even and flat.
7. Place the dish in the refrigerator until the mixture hardens.
8. When it is hard, remove the dish from the refrigerator and cut into squares.

Yield: 10-12 squares

Chocomalo Squares

1½ cups	**chocolate chips**	**375 mL**
1 cup	**marshmallows**	**250 mL**
1½ cups	**Rice Krispies (or Cherrios, Cornflakes, etc.)**	**375 mL**

1. Grease an 8" (20 cm) square baking dish.
2. Take a double boiler and place hot water in the bottom pan and chocolate chips in the top pan.
3. Melt the chocolate in the double boiler, on the stove, over medium heat.
4. When the chocolate has melted, remove the double boiler from the heat and add marshmallows.
5. Continue stirring with the top pan still over the saucepan of hot water, until the marshmallows have mostly melted.
6. Add the Rice Krispies, 1 cup (250 mL) at a time, mixing in well, and add a bit more cereal if it is not thick enough.
7. When mixture is well mixed, remove the top saucepan and pour Rice Krispie mixture into baking dish.
8. Use the back of a fork to flatten the mixture evenly.
9. Place the dish in the freezer for 10 minutes.
10. Cut the cake into squares and then place the dish back in the freezer.
11. After 5 more minutes, remove the squares from the freezer and from the dish. Enjoy every bite!

Yield: 9 large squares

Crunchies

¼ cup	**butter**	**60 mL**
1 tbsp.	**corn syrup**	**15 mL**
½ tsp.	**baking soda**	**2 mL**
⅓ cup	**all-purpose flour**	**75 mL**
⅓ cup	**Rice Krispies**	**75 mL**
⅓ cup	**brown sugar**	**75 mL**
⅓ cup	**rolled oats**	**75 mL**
⅓ cup	**raisins (optional)**	**75 mL**

1. Preheat the oven to 320°F (160°C).
2. Grease an 8" (20 cm) square baking pan.
3. In a small saucepan, over medium heat, melt the butter and corn syrup.
4. When the butter has melted, remove from the heat and stir in the baking soda.
5. In another bowl, mix together the flour, Rice Krispies, sugar, oats and raisins, if using.
6. Add the dry ingredients to the butter mixture and mix well.
7. Pour the Rice Krispie mixture into the pan, spreading it evenly with the back of a fork.
8. Bake the Crunchies for 25 minutes, then turn the oven off and leave them in for 5-10 minutes more.
9. Remove the cake from the oven and cut into squares, giving them time to cool before eating.

Yield: 9 large squares

One-Dish Brownies

The reason these are called one-dish is because you only use one dish, which means there is much less to wash up!

⅓ cup	**butter**	**75 mL**
⅓ cup	**white sugar**	**75 mL**
⅓ cup	**brown sugar**	**75 mL**
¼ cup	**cocoa**	**60 mL**
1	**egg**	**1**
⅓ cup	**flour**	**75 mL**
½ tsp.	**baking powder**	**2 mL**
½ tsp.	**vanilla extract**	**2 mL**
⅓ cup	**chopped walnuts**	**75 mL**
⅓ cup	**chocolate chips**	**75 mL**

1. Preheat oven to 350°F (180°C).
2. Grease an 8" (20 cm) square baking dish.
3. Put butter into the dish and microwave for a few seconds, until it has melted.
4. Add white and brown sugars and mix well.
5. Add the cocoa and egg and continue mixing well.
6. Sift in the flour and baking powder.
7. Mix in the vanilla extract and chopped nuts.
8. Finally, add half of the chocolate chips and mix in gently, then sprinkle the other half on top.
9. Place the dish in the oven for 35-40 minutes, or until a toothpick inserted in the center comes out clean (see baking hint on page 11).
10. Remove from the oven, cut into squares and allow to cool.

Yield: 9 large squares

Hello Dolly Bars

These are magical – so good and so easy!

½ cup	**butter**	**125 mL**
1½ cups	**graham wafer crumbs**	**375 mL**
10 oz.	**can sweetened condensed milk**	**300 mL**
1 cup	**semisweet chocolate chips**	**250 mL**
1⅓ cups	**flaked coconut**	**325 mL**
1 cup	**chopped nuts**	**250 mL**

1. Preheat the oven to 350°F (180°C).
2. Place the butter in a 9 x 13" (23 x 33 cm) baking pan and put it in the oven.
3. Once the butter is melted, remove the pan from the oven and sprinkle graham crumbs over the bottom of the pan to form a base.
4. Pour the condensed milk evenly over the base (if you drizzle it over the back of a spoon or a fork, it won't make holes in the base.)
5. Sprinkle the chocolate chips, then coconut and nuts evenly over the condensed milk.
6. Bake in the oven for 25-30 minutes, or until golden brown color.
7. When ready, remove from the oven and allow to cool.
8. Cut into 24 bars.

Yield: 24 bars

Lemon Squares

This is unbelievably delicious, it is one of my very favorite recipes.

Shortbread Base:

1 cup	**all-purpose flour**	**250 mL**
½ cup	**butter**	**125 mL**
⅓ cup	**confectioner's sugar**	**75 mL**

Lemon Topping:

2	**eggs**	**2**
1 cup	**sugar**	**250 mL**
5 tbsp.	**flour**	**75 mL**
3 tbsp.	**lemon juice**	**45 mL**

1. Preheat the oven to 350°F (180°C).
2. In a medium bowl, mix together the flour, butter and confectioner's sugar with an electric beater until the mixture forms a dough.
3. Grease an 8" (20 cm) square baking dish and press the dough evenly over the bottom of the dish to form a base.
4. Put baking dish in the oven for 25 minutes, until the base is a golden brown color.
5. In a small bowl, combine the eggs, sugar, flour and lemon juice with the electric beater. Mix well.
6. When the lemon mixture appears very thick and creamy, pour it over the baked base.
7. Return the dish to the oven and bake for another 25-30 minutes.
8. Remove the dish from the oven and allow it to cool.
9. Sprinkle a little additional confectioner's sugar over the top and cut the cake into squares.

Yield: 9 large squares or 12 smaller squares

M
delightful
DESSERTS

Chocolate Mousse

A very special dessert, it is always nice to serve mousse with a little whipped cream on top.

1¼ cups	**dark unsweetened chocolate chips**	**300 mL**
5	**eggs, separated**	**5**
2 tsp.	**vanilla extract**	**10 mL**
2 tsp.	**instant coffee, dissolved in 2 tbsp. (30 mL) hot water**	**10 mL**
1 cup+2 tbsp.	**whipping cream**	**280 mL**

1. In a double boiler over medium heat, put boiling water in the bottom pan and put the chocolate chips in the top pan.
2. Melt the chocolate chips while stirring.
3. When chocolate chips have melted, remove from the heat.
4. Separate* the eggs, putting the whites in 1 bowl and yolks in another.
5. Beat the egg yolks.
6. Let the chocolate cool, then mix in the beaten egg yolks.
7. Mix in the vanilla extract and dissolved coffee solution.
8. In a deep narrow bowl, beat the cream with an electric mixer, until it is thick and creamy.
9. Fold the cream gently into the chocolate mixture.
10. Wash the beaters very carefully. In another deep narrow bowl, beat the egg whites until they are stiff and glossy.
11. Fold the egg whites into the chocolate mixture, a little at a time, until they are well mixed through.
12. Refrigerate the covered mousse for 2-3 hours, until it has set.

Serves: 6-8 good portions

*See hint about separating eggs on page 6.

Beating Egg Whites: Use a large deep bowl; it must be clean and grease-free, glass or stainless steel is best. Egg whites that are at room temperature will give the greatest volume.

Dreamy Ice Cream

Ice cream worth daydreaming about.

4	**eggs**	**4**
10 oz.	**can sweetened condensed milk**	**300 mL**
1 cup	**whipping cream**	**250 mL**
1 tbsp.	**vanilla extract**	**15 mL**

1. Break each egg separately into a small bowl to ensure that the eggs are usable and then put them into a big bowl and beat well.
2. Add the condensed milk and continue beating until the eggs and condensed milk are well combined.
3. In a deep narrow bowl, beat the cream until it is thick and firm.
4. Fold the cream into the egg mixture, mixing gently.
5. Finally, fold in the vanilla extract.
6. Pour the ice cream into a deep dish and freeze until it is hard. Stir every 30 minutes for a smoother texture.

Yield: Enough for 10-15 people, depending on scoop size.

Variation: Add 1 cup (250 mL) of chocolate chips.

Banana Treat

A great reward after a long, hard day in school.

1	**banana**	**1**
1	**big scoop of ice cream or frozen yogurt**	**1**
½ cup	**granola**	**125 mL**
2 tbsp.	**honey**	**30 mL**
dash	**cinnamon**	**dash**

1. Peel the banana and slice into a bowl.
2. Top the banana with the following in the order given: 1 scoop of ice cream, granola and honey.
3. Sprinkle some cinnamon over the honey and dig in.

Serves: 1

Berry Shortcake

Strawberry Filling:

2½ cups	**fresh strawberries**	**625 mL**
3 tbsp.	**sugar**	**45 mL**

Topping:

1 cup	**whipping cream**	**250 mL**
1 tsp.	**sugar**	**5 mL**
1 tsp.	**vanilla extract**	**5 mL**
6-8	**tea biscuits or berry cups***	**6-8**

1. To prepare the filling, wash the strawberries, remove the hulls and then slice them into a bowl.
2. Sprinkle sugar over them and allow them to stand.
3. To prepare the topping, combine the cream, sugar and vanilla extract in a deep narrow bowl.
4. Using an electric mixer, beat until it forms a stiff mixture. Be careful not to overbeat or you will make butter!
5. To put it all together, cut the tea biscuits in half or use the berry cups as they are.
6. Put the strawberry filling on top of the bottom half of the biscuit or fill the berry cup.
7. Put the top half of the biscuit on top.
8. Drop a big blob of the whipped cream on top of the biscuit.
9. EAT AT ONCE!

Serves: 6-8

Variation: Substitute fresh blueberries or raspberries for the strawberries. You won't even have to slice them!

*Ready made tea biscuits or berry cups are available commercially.

Minicheesecakes

Creamy and versatile.

	Sweet Cookie Dough, page 26, uncooked	
¾ cup	**cream cheese**	**175 mL**
⅓ cup	**cream**	**75 mL**
¼ cup	**sugar**	**60 mL**
1	**egg**	**1**
½ tsp.	**vanilla extract**	**2 mL**
pinch	**salt**	**pinch**
1 tbsp.	**flour**	**15 mL**

1. Preheat the oven to 350°F (180°F).
2. Dust a board and rolling pin with flour and roll out the dough until it is thin and smooth.
3. Take a big glass and cut out circles in the dough to fit the bottom of a muffin pan.
4. Grease the muffin pan and line each cup with a dough circle.
5. In a medium bowl, combine the cream cheese, cream and sugar, and beat with an electric beater until smooth and creamy.
6. Mix in the egg, vanilla extract and salt.
7. Lastly, sift the flour into the bowl and mix thoroughly with a metal spoon.
8. Spoon the batter into the dough-lined muffin cups so they are ¾ full.
9. Bake for 30 minutes and then switch the oven off, leaving them in for another 10 minutes.
10. Remove cheesecakes from the oven and allow to cool before taking them out of the muffin pan.

Yield: 10 minicheesecakes

Variations: For a shortcut you can use commercial vanilla or chocolate wafers instead of the cookie dough. Place a wafer in the bottom of each muffin pan and proceed with step 5. Baked Cheesecakes can be topped with sliced fresh fruit or your favorite fruit sauces.

Apple Crumble

3	**apples or 19 oz. (540 mL) can apple pie filling**	**3**
	cinnamon	
½ cup	**butter**	**125 mL**
¾ cup	**brown sugar**	**175 mL**
1½ cups	**all-purpose flour**	**375 mL**

1. Preheat the oven to 350°F (180°C).
2. Peel, core and halve the apples and then grate them.
3. In a microwave-safe dish, place the apples in the microwave on high for 2 minutes, until they are partially cooked.
4. Grease an 8" (20 cm) square baking dish and cover the bottom of the dish with the apples.
5. Sprinkle a bit of cinnamon over the apples.
6. In a small saucepan, melt the butter and sugar over medium heat.
7. When the butter has melted and the sugar has dissolved, remove it from the heat and pour it into a bowl. Let it cool a little.
8. Sift the flour over the butter mixture.
9. Using your hands, mix the ingredients together until you have a crumbly dough.
10. When it is properly mixed through, cover the apples with the crumbs.
11. Sprinkle some cinnamon on top of the crumbs.
12. Place the dish in the oven for 30 minutes, or until it is golden.
13. When it is ready, remove the crumble from the oven and allow it to cool a little.
14. Serve it warm with a scoop of ice cream.

Serves: 8

Variations: Use your imagination here. Try your favorite fruit or fruit pie fillings instead of apples: peaches, pears, blueberries, rhubarb, plums, etc.

CANDY LANE
LOLLYPOP CRES
sweet
STREET

Cornflake Globs

Absolutely delicious, unbelievably chocolatey and extraordinary mouth-watering treats.

2 tbsp.	**margarine**	**30 mL**
⅔ cup	**confectioner's (icing) sugar**	**150 mL**
3 cups	**regular-size marshmallows**	**750 mL**
1 cup	**chocolate chips**	**250 mL**
4 cups	**cornflakes**	**1 L**

1. Melt the margarine in a large saucepan, over medium heat.
2. Keeping the saucepan over medium heat, add confectioner's sugar and mix well.
3. Stir in the marshmallows and continue to stir while they melt.
4. Add half of the chocolate chips, allow to melt and mix with the marshmallow mixture.
5. When most of the chocolate chips have melted, add the cornflakes a cup at a time. Be sure to mix each cup in well before adding the next cup.
6. Add the other half of the chocolate chips and remove the saucepan from the heat.
7. Grease a cookie sheet and, using a spoon, place globs of the cornflake mixture on it.
8. Place in the freezer for 10-15 minutes or let them set for longer at room temperature.

Yield: 10 large globs

Nuts about Popcorn

2 cups	**unpopped popcorn**	**500 mL**
1 tbsp.	**butter**	**15 mL**
3 tbsp.	**honey**	**45 mL**
3 tbsp.	**sugar**	**45 mL**
½ cup	**mixed nuts**	**125 mL**

1. Pop the popcorn, let it cool and then remove any kernels that have not popped.
2. Melt the butter, honey and sugar in a large saucepan over medium heat.
3. When the butter mixture has melted and the sugar has dissolved, stir in the nuts.
4. Continue stirring until the mixture becomes golden and the nuts appear crystallized (coated with sugar crystals).
5. Remove the pan from the heat, cool the syrup **slightly** so popcorn doesn't wilt; add the popcorn and mix. Be very careful; the syrup is burning hot*.
6. Grease a cookie sheet and spread the popcorn out evenly.
7. When it is cool, break it into chunks and enjoy!

Yield: Enough for 8-10 people

*Boiling syrup can be very dangerous. DO NOT attempt this recipe unless an adult is there to supervise.

Truffles

These are sensational peanut butter truffles.

½ cup	**crunchy peanut butter**	**125 mL**
2 tbsp.	**soft butter**	**30 mL**
½ cup	**confectioner's (icing) sugar**	**125 mL**
¾ cup	**chocolate chips**	**175 mL**

1. Mix the peanut butter, butter and confectioner's sugar in a bowl.
2. When it is well mixed, make small balls.
3. Set the balls on a cookie sheet or board covered with wax paper.
4. Place the board in the freezer for 1-2 hours, until the balls are well chilled.
5. When the balls are ready, melt the chocolate in the top half of a double boiler with boiling water in the bottom, and the double boiler over medium heat.
6. Remove the balls from the freezer. Spear them with a skewer and dip them, 1 at a time, into the melted chocolate.
7. After dipping each ball, return it to the waxed paper-covered cookie sheet.
8. After dipping all the balls, place the sheet in the refrigerator to allow the chocolate to harden.
9. After 15-20 minutes, remove from the refrigerator.
10. Allow truffles 5-10 minutes to come to room temperature and then treasure every mouthful!

Yield: 1 dozen

Almond Bark

These make great gifts if you can bear to part with them.

2/3 cup	**white or dark chocolate chips**	**150 mL**
1/2 cup	**whole almonds**	**125 mL**
2 tsp.	**butter**	**10 mL**

1. Melt the chocolate chips in the top pot of a double boiler, with hot water in the bottom pot, set over medium heat.
2. When the chocolate has mostly melted, remove the double boiler from the heat.
3. Place the almonds and butter in a bowl and heat in the microwave for 2-3 minutes on high.
4. Add the almonds to the melted chocolate and mix well.
5. Line a baking sheet with waxed paper.
6. Pour the chocolate almond mixture onto the waxed paper and spread it out evenly.
7. Place the baking sheet in the freezer for 45 minutes.
8. When the chocolate is hard, break it into small pieces and store in an airtight container.

Yields: a variety of sizes and shapes

Chocolate Caramels

1 cup	**unsalted butter**	**250 mL**
½ cup	**semisweet chocolate chips**	**125 mL**
10 oz.	**can sweetened condensed milk**	**30 mL**
¼ cup	**corn syrup**	**60 mL**
2¼ cups	**brown sugar**	**550 mL**

1. Grease an oblong or square baking pan.
2. Combine the butter, chocolate, condensed milk, corn syrup and sugar in a large, heavy saucepan.
3. Place the saucepan over medium heat and mix with a wooden spoon.
4. Keep stirring until the chocolate has melted, and the mixture comes to a boil*.
5. Turn the heat down to medium-low and cook slowly, stirring continuously.
6. Keep stirring over medium-low heat for 25-30 minutes. It is important to keep stirring because candy burns easily.
7. When the candy reaches a thick consistency it is cooked.
8. Remove the saucepan from the heat.
9. Pour the mixture into the baking pan and let it cool on the kitchen counter. For quicker results, or in the summer when the house is warmer, cool in the refrigerator.
10. After 1½ hours of cooling, cut the candy into squares and leave it in the pan for another 30 minutes.
11. When the candy has completely cooled and hardened, you can remove it from the pan and place it in an airtight container.

Yield: 30 squares

*Boiling syrup can be very dangerous. DO NOT attempt this recipe unless an adult is there to supervise.

Fabulous Fudge

2¼ cups	**sugar**	**550 mL**
¾ cup	**ideal milk**	**175 mL**
16	**large marshmallows**	**16**
¼ cup	**butter**	**60 mL**
¼ tsp.	**salt**	**1 mL**
1¼ cups	**chocolate chips**	**300 mL**
1 tsp.	**vanilla extract**	**5 mL**

1. In a heavy saucepan, over medium heat, combine the sugar, milk, marshmallows, butter and salt.
2. Bring to a boil, stirring constantly, and boil for 5 minutes.*
3. After 5 minutes, remove the saucepan from the heat and stir in the chocolate chips.
4. When the chocolate chips have melted, add the vanilla extract and stir.
5. Grease an 8" (20 cm) square baking pan and pour the fudge mixture into the pan.
7. Level the mixture so that it is smooth and even.
8. Allow the fudge to cool and then cut it into squares.

Yield: 30 pieces of fudge

*Boiling syrup can be very dangerous. Do NOT attempt this recipe unless an adult is there to supervise.

worlds
GREATEST
recipes

Rösti

Switzerland

5	**medium potatoes, scrubbed but not peeled**	**5**
1	**onion, peeled and chopped**	**1**
	salt	
	pepper	
3 tbsp.	**vegetable oil**	**45 mL**

1. Place the potatoes in a medium saucepan and cover them with cold water.
2. Bring the water to a boil by placing the saucepan over high heat and cook the potatoes until they are tender, about 20-25 minutes.
3. When potatoes are ready, remove them from the heat, drain and allow them to cool.
4. Grate the cooled potatoes into a bowl, add the chopped onion and salt and pepper to taste.
5. Heat the oil in a 10" (25 cm) frying pan over medium heat.
6. Add the potato mixture, pressing it down with the back of a spoon.
7. Allow the rösti to fry for 10 minutes, or until the bottom side is golden brown.
8. Turn the rösti over by inverting a plate over the frying pan. Turn the plate and frying pan over together so the rösti is on the plate, browned side up. Slide the rösti back into the frying pan, uncooked side down. Fry until the bottom side is the same golden brown as the top.
9. When both sides are golden brown, turn the rösti over onto a plate and, using your hands, break it into 4 pieces.

Serves: 4

Scotch Shortbread

Scotland – The authentic Scottish Shortbread.

1 cup	**butter**	**250 mL**
½ cup	**superfine (berry) sugar**	**125 mL**
2½ cups	**flour**	**625 mL**
1 tsp.	**almond extract**	**5 mL**
½ tsp.	**vanilla extract**	**2 mL**
½ cup	**cornstarch**	**125 mL**

1. Preheat the oven to 350°F (180°C).
2. In a small saucepan over medium heat melt the butter.
3. In a large bowl, combine the melted butter and the sugar. Using an electric mixer, beat until light and creamy.
4. Sift the flour into the bowl and continue beating.
5. Add the almond and vanilla extracts and mix well.
6. Lastly, add the cornstarch and mix until it is well combined.
7. Grease a 10½ x 15" (25 x 38 cm) jelly roll pan.
8. Put the dough into the pan and press it down until it is level.
9. Using a fork, lightly prick holes all over the dough.
11. Bake on the middle oven rack for 20-25 minutes, until pale brown.
12. Remove from the oven and cut while hot.
13. When the shortbread has cooled, remove it from the pan and store in an airtight container.

Yield: 20 cookies

Koulourakia

Greece

½ cup	**butter**	**125 mL**
½ cup	**sugar**	**125 mL**
2	**eggs**	**2**
1 tsp.	**vanilla extract**	**5 mL**
2½ cups	**all-purpose flour**	**625 mL**
1½ tsp.	**baking powder**	**7 mL**
pinch	**salt**	**pinch**
2 tbsp.	**milk**	**30 mL**

1. Preheat the oven to 350°F (180°C).
2. In a medium bowl, with an electric mixer, cream the butter and the sugar until it is light and creamy.
3. Add the eggs and the vanilla extract and continue mixing.
4. After a minute of mixing, add 2 cups (500 mL) of flour, 1 cup (250 mL) at a time, leaving the ½ cup (125 mL) flour for later.
5. Add the baking powder and salt and continue mixing until all the ingredients are well combined.
6. If the mixture is still too soft, add the ½ cup (125 mL) flour.
7. Dust a board with flour and knead the dough on the board.
8. Take golf ball-sized portions of the dough and shape the dough into rings or twists, twisting 2 pieces of dough together.
9. Place the cookies on a greased cookie sheet. You can brush the cookies with milk to help them turn a nice golden color.
10. Bake them on the middle oven rack for 20 minutes, or until they are golden brown.
11. Remove the cookies from the oven when they are ready and allow them to cool before eating.

Yield: 3 dozen cookies

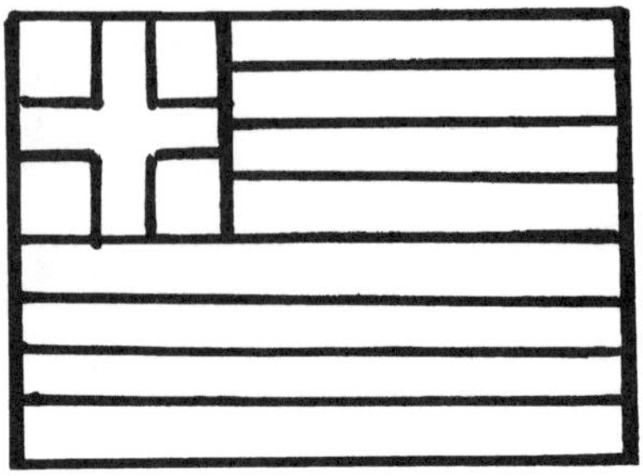

Aussie Oatcakes

Australia

3 tbsp.	**butter**	**45 mL**
2 tbsp.	**brown sugar**	**30 mL**
¼ tsp.	**baking soda**	**1 mL**
½ tsp.	**ginger**	**2 mL**
1 tsp.	**water**	**5 mL**
¾ cup	**rolled oats**	**175 mL**

1. Preheat the oven to 325°F (160°C).
2. Mix the butter and the brown sugar together, using an electric mixer.
3. Add the baking soda, ginger and water and continue mixing.
4. Finally, add the rolled oats and mix for another minute.
5. Divide the dough-like mixture into 5 equal portions.
6. Grease a cookie sheet and place the portions on it, allowing space between them for spreading.
7. Using the palm of your hand, flatten the portions and mold each into a square shape.
8. Set the cookie sheet on the middle oven rack for 12-15 minutes.
9. When the oatcakes are a light brown color, remove them from the oven.
10. Allow oatcakes to cool slightly before eating.

Yield: 5 oatcakes

American Cookies

United States – The All-American Chocolate Chip Cookie.

½ cup	**butter**	**125 mL**
½ cup	**brown sugar**	**125 mL**
½ cup	**white sugar**	**125 mL**
1	**egg, well beaten**	**1**
½ tsp.	**vanilla extract**	**2 mL**
1 cup	**flour**	**250 mL**
1 tsp.	**baking powder**	**5 mL**
¼ tsp.	**salt**	**1 mL**
1 cup	**chocolate chips**	**250 mL**

1. Preheat the oven to 350°F (180°C).
2. In a medium bowl, using an electric mixer, cream the butter and sugars until the mixture is light and creamy.
3. Break an egg into a small bowl and beat well.
4. Add the egg and the vanilla extract to the creamy mixture and stir well.
5. Next, sift the flour, baking powder and salt over the butter mixture.
6. Continue mixing with the electric mixer until the ingredients are well combined. If the mixture is too thin, you can add some extra flour. The batter should not be runny – it should have a consistency like yogurt.
7. Finally, add the chocolate chips and stir them in with a metal spoon.
8. Lightly grease a cookie sheet and drop the mixture by spoonfuls onto the greased cookie sheet, making sure you leave them enough space for cookies to expand.
9. Bake the cookies on the middle oven rack for 12 minutes.
10. Remove cookies from the oven and allow them to cool before eating.

Yield: 2 dozen large cookies

Koeksisters

South Africa

Syrup:

2 cups	**sugar**	**500 mL**
1 cup	**water**	**250 mL**
2 tsp.	**lemon juice**	**10 mL**

Dough:

1¼ cups	**flour**	**300 mL**
pinch	**salt**	**pinch**
2 tsp.	**baking powder**	**10 mL**
2 tbsp.+2 tsp.	**butter**	**40 mL**
1	**egg**	**1**
½ cup	**milk**	**125 mL**
	vegetable oil for deep frying	

1. In a large heavy saucepan, combine the sugar, water and lemon juice and stir over medium-high heat.
2. When the sugar has dissolved and the syrup begins to boil, stop stirring and boil for 7 minutes*.
3. Remove the syrup from the heat and place the saucepan in the refrigerator until it is needed.
4. To make the dough, sift the flour, salt and baking powder into a large bowl.
5. In a small bowl, melt the butter in the microwave on high for a few seconds.
6. Pour the melted butter into the bowl with the dry ingredients.
7. Rub in the butter until the mixture resembles bread crumbs.
8. Add the egg and milk and knead well, until the crumbs become a smooth dough.
9. Divide the dough into 16 equal portions and sprinkle some flour over a board.
10. Take 1 portion and divide it into 3 pieces.
11. Roll each portion with the palm of your hand so that it resembles a small pencil.

Koeksisters

Continued

12. Braid the 3 separate pieces, ensuring that the ends will not come undone (pinch them together tightly).
13. Place a deep frying pan over high heat or use an electric deep-fryer if you have one. Heat oil to 365°F (185°C).
14. Pour enough oil into a frying pan to allow you to deep-fry the braided pieces of dough.
15. Place 1 braid in the frying pan and when it begins to fry, add a few more.
16. Keep turning the braids until they are a golden color.
17. Line a baking sheet with paper towels and place the cooked braids on it to drain off excess oil.
18. When all the braids are cooked, remove the syrup from the refrigerator and place the saucepan next to the braids.
19. Place a sheet of waxed paper over another baking sheet. Carefully dip the braids into the syrup, coating them completely in syrup.
20. Place the coated braids on the waxed paper and eat as soon as you can – they are absolutely scrumptious!

Yield: 16 braids

*Boiling syrup and deep-frying can be very dangerous. DO NOT attempt this recipe unless an adult is there to supervise.

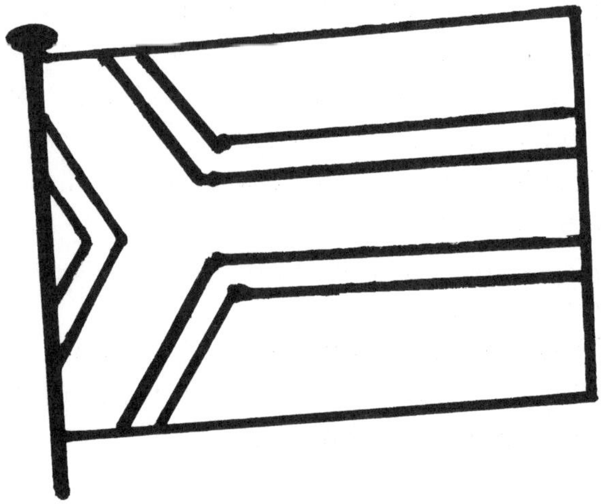

Play Dough*

The cooked method.

2 cups	**flour**	**500 mL**
1 cup	**salt**	**250 mL**
4 tsp.	**cream of tartar**	**20 mL**
2 cups	**water**	**500 mL**
2 tbsp.	**vegetable oil**	**30 mL**
	food coloring (optional)	

1. Measure all of the ingredients into a large heavy pot.
2. Put the pot over medium-high heat and keep stirring.
3. When the dough becomes thick and begins to boil, remove the pot from the heat.
4. When the dough has cooled, put the dough in an airtight container and keep the container in the refrigerator.

Yield: 2 cups (500 mL)

Play Dough*

The no-cook method.

2 cups	**self-raising flour**	**500 mL**
2 tbsp.	**alum**	**30 mL**
2 tbsp.	**salt**	**30 mL**
2 tbsp.	**vegetable oil**	**30 mL**
1⅓ cups	**boiling water**	**325 mL**

1. Mix the ingredients together in a large bowl.
2. Use your hands to knead the dough until it is smooth and pliable.
3. Store in an airtight container.

Yield: 1½-2 cups (375-500 mL)

*These recipes are not intended to be eaten.

Index

Share *Cook & Color* with a friend

Order *Cook & Color* at $6.95 per book plus $3.00 (total order) for shipping and handling.

Number of copies ______________________ x $6.95 = $ ________

Postage and handling (total order) ______________________ = $ 3.00

Subtotal ______________________ = $ ________

In Canada add 7% GST ______________________ (Subtotal x .07) = $ ________

Total enclosed ______________________ = $ ________

U.S. and international orders payable in U.S. funds./ Price is subject to change.

NAME: ______________________

STREET: ______________________

CITY: ______________________ PROV./STATE ______________________

COUNTRY ______________________ POSTAL CODE/ZIP ______________________

Please make cheque or money order payable to: **Cooking for Kids**
1012 Rick Hansen Crescent
Kingston, Ontario
K7P 2M8

For fund raising or volume purchases, contact **Cooking for Kids** for volume rates.
Please allow 2-3 weeks for delivery

Share *Cook & Color* with a friend

Order *Cook & Color* at $6.95 per book plus $3.00 (total order) for shipping and handling.

Number of copies ______________________ x $6.95 = $ ________

Postage and handling (total order) ______________________ = $ 3.00

Subtotal ______________________ = $ ________

In Canada add 7% GST ______________________ (Subtotal x .07) = $ ________

Total enclosed ______________________ = $ ________

U.S. and international orders payable in U.S. funds./ Price is subject to change.

NAME: ______________________

STREET: ______________________

CITY: ______________________ PROV./STATE ______________________

COUNTRY ______________________ POSTAL CODE/ZIP ______________________

Please make cheque or money order payable to: **Cooking for Kids**
1012 Rick Hansen Crescent
Kingston, Ontario
K7P 2M8

For fund raising or volume purchases, contact **Cooking for Kids** for volume rates.
Please allow 2-3 weeks for delivery